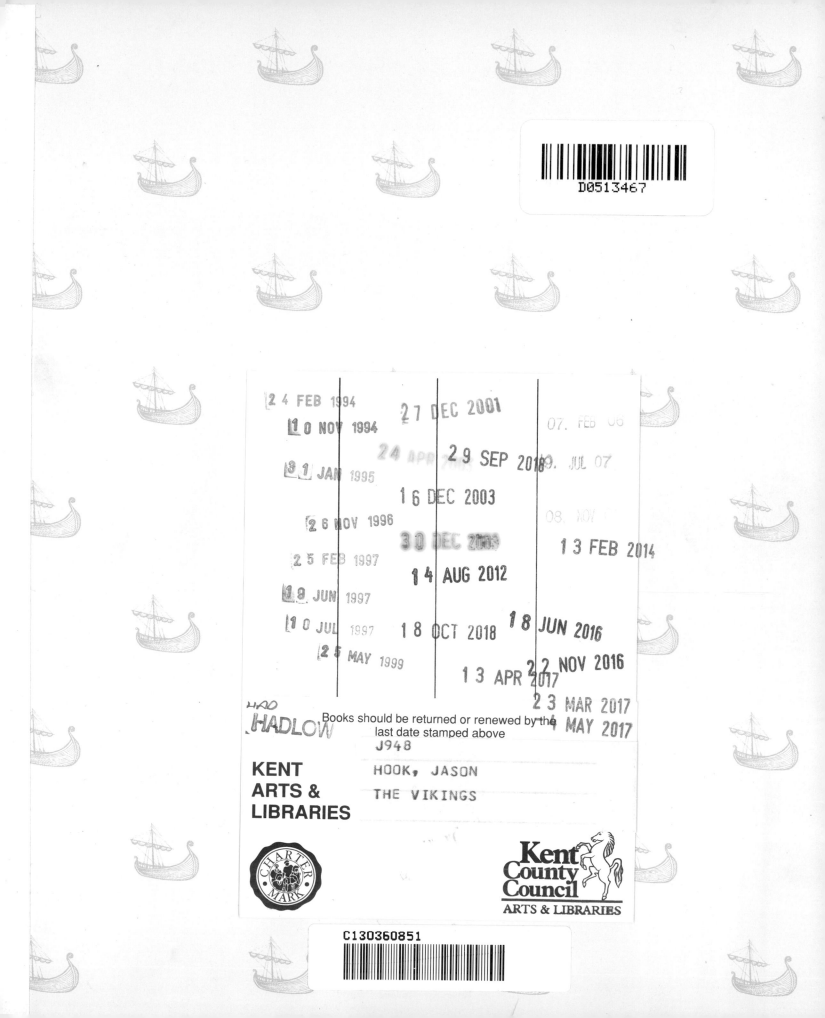

# THE
# VIKINGS

Jason Hook

Wayland

# Look into the Past

The Anglo-Saxons
The Aztecs
The Egyptians
The Greeks
The Normans
The Romans
The Victorians
The Vikings

Series editor: Joanna Housley
Series designer: David West
Book designer: Joyce Chester

First published in 1993 by Wayland (Publishers) Limited
61 Western Road, Hove, East Sussex, BN3 1JD, England

**British Library Cataloguing in Publication Data**
   Hook, Jason
   Vikings. – (Look into the Past series)
   I. Title II. Series
   948.02

ISBN 0 7502 0726 4

Typeset by DJS Fotoset Ltd, Sussex, England.
Printed and bound in Italy by L.E.G.O. S.p.A.,
Vicenza, Italy.

**Picture acknowledgements**
The publishers wish to thank the following for providing the
photographs for this book: Ancient Art and Architecture
Collection 11 (top); British Library 27 (right); C M Dixon 6,
7 (bottom, Ashmolean Museum, Oxford), 10 (right,
Museum of National Antiquities, Stockholm), 11 (bottom),
13 (top, Museum of National Antiquities, Stockholm), 15
(both; right University Historical Museum, Oslo), 16, 17
(bottom), 19 (top, National Museum, Copenhagen; left), 21
(bottom left and top right, Viking Ship Museum, Bygdoy),
23 (both, Museum of National Antiquities, Stockholm), 23
(both, Museum of National Antiquities, Stockholm), 24
(British Museum), 29 (bottom); E T Archive 27 (left,
Bodleian Library); Werner Forman Archive 5 (top), 6
(Statens Historiska Museum, Stockholm), 7 (top, Stofnun
Arna Magnussonar a Islandi, Iceland), 8 (Universitets
Oldsaksamling, Oslo), 9 (both, top Statens Historiska
Museum, Stockholm, bottom, Viking Ship Museum,
Bygdoy), 12, 14 (left), 18 (Statens Historiska Museum,
Stockholm), 20 (Viking Ship Museum, Bygdoy), 21 (top left,
Viking Ship Museum, Bygdoy), 22 (Statens Historiska
Museum, Stockholm), 25 (right, National Museum,
Copenhagen), 26 (both, British Museum), 29 (top); Michael
Holford 25 (left, Staten Historiska Museum, Stockholm), 28
(Musée de Bayeux); York Archaeological Trust 5 (bottom),
10 (left), 13 (bottom), 17 (top 3).
Map artwork on page 4 by Jenny Hughes.

# CONTENTS

Words that appear in **bold italic** in the text are explained in the glossary on page 30.

# WHO WERE THE VIKINGS?

Over one thousand years ago, a race of pirates, traders, explorers and settlers swarmed across Europe with such fury that their influence is felt even today. They were the Vikings: fearless warriors who discovered new lands, founded cities, and invaded foreign countries. They were so successful that their language and descendants still survive in many countries today.

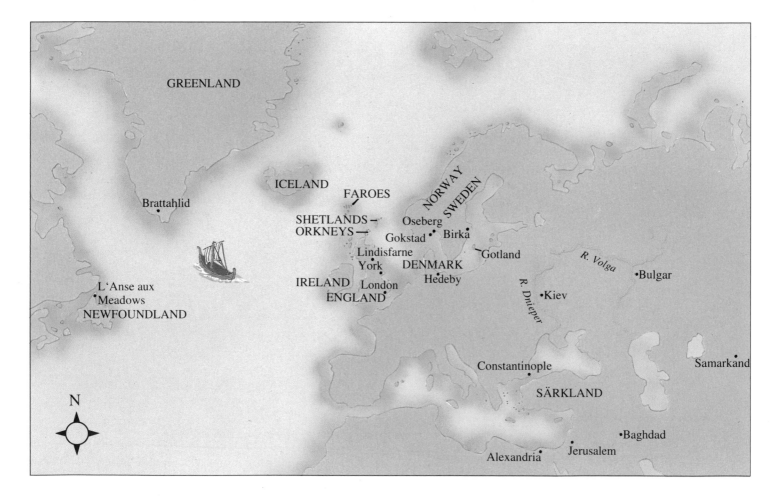

The name 'Viking' describes those people who came from three countries of **Scandinavia** – Norway, Denmark and Sweden – between 793 and 1066. This map shows how far the Vikings travelled on their many raids and voyages. Sailing east to Arab lands and west as far as America, the Vikings knew more of the world than anyone before them.

◄ In those days, it was quicker to travel by water than by land – across Sweden's many lakes, around the coasts of Denmark's 500 islands, or along the deep, narrow *fjords* of Norway, like this one at Sogne. So, the Scandinavians had a long sailing *tradition*. When the population outgrew their farming lands, they sailed for foreign seas and the Viking Age began.

On 8 June 793, Vikings from Norway landed at Holy Island, off the coast of north-east England. They looted Lindisfarne monastery and killed its monks.
This ninth-century memorial stone shows these first Viking raiders. ▼

▲ *Archaeologists* can learn a lot about the Vikings by studying *artefacts* that have been found in areas where they lived. The Vikings buried weapons, jewellery, even entire ships with their dead, preserving important *relics* of their history. This carving from a cart buried in Oseberg, Norway, suggests the appearance of the Vikings whose raids terrorized Europe for some 250 years.

# THE VIKING LANGUAGE

The Vikings spoke a language called Old Norse. Some modern towns have names formed from Norse words, showing that they grew from Viking settlements. The word 'by' is Norse for 'town'. So, in England, the place-name 'Danby' originally meant 'Dane town', and the word 'by-law' means 'law of the town'. English words like 'them', 'take' and 'die' are also of Viking origin.

Having no pens or paper, the Vikings carved thin letters called runes into wood and stone. Using a 16-rune alphabet called the futhorc, they carved tombstones and jewellery with words which can still be read today. This stone shows the pre-Viking futhorc of 24 runes.

Rune stones were put up to mark graves and bridges throughout the Viking world. This eleventh-century stone from Uppland, Sweden, reads: 'Torsten caused this monument to be made in memory of Sven, his father, and of Tore, his brother, who were in Greece, and of Ingletora, his mother.' Rune stones like this one, and the places where they have been found, show us how widely the Vikings travelled. ▼

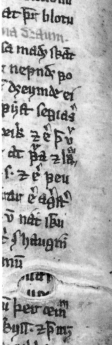

▲ The Sagas are another source of Viking history. They are tales based on true Viking adventures, which were beautifully written in thirteenth-century Iceland. This picture from the Saga of St Olaf shows the death of Olaf Haraldsson, or Olaf the Stout, King of Norway from 1015 to 1030. Olaf, who forced his people to adopt Christianity, became patron saint of Scandinavia.

# THE LONGSHIP

The Vikings became masters of the seas by building the finest ships of the time. With *keels* to steady them, Viking longships could sail swiftly across open sea, or be rowed into the shallowest waters. No one was safe from sudden Viking attack.

Some longships had carved *figureheads*. Can you imagine what the figurehead would have been on a ship named 'Long Serpent' or 'Great Dragon'? Other ships had bronze *vanes* like this one, which later became a weather-vane on Heggen Church in Norway. Can you make out the shapes of dragons engraved on it? The dents are thought to have been caused by flying arrows.

This longship was dug up in Norway in 1880. It had been preserved in a clay burial ground since the ninth century. It is made of overlapping, curved oak timbers. Can you see the holes where the oars would have been? Found with the 23-metre-long ship were sixty-four black and gold shields, which would once have been displayed along the ship's rails. ▶

▲ Although no canvas sails survive, the square sails of Viking ships are shown on coins, which were first *minted* in Scandinavia in the ninth century. These coins were found at Birka, Sweden, one of several market towns built up from the trade brought by Viking ships. The coins show a knorr, which was a broad, slow merchant ship.

# TRADE

**As well as raiding, Vikings also traded peacefully with distant *empires*. Trade created Scandinavia's first towns, like Birka, where archaeologists now find buried hoards of foreign silks, glass and precious metals.**

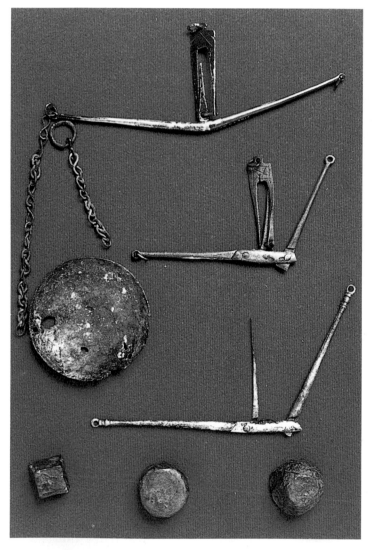

Swedish merchants sailed down the Volga and Dnieper rivers through Russia to the Black, Caspian and Mediterranean Seas. They ruled over Kiev, and became known as the 'Rus' – after which Russia is named. These Vikings traded furs, iron, wax, honey, even slaves, for Chinese silk and treasured Arabian silver. 85,000 Arabic coins like these have been dug up in Scandinavia, revealing the dates and sources of Viking trade. ▼

▲ Early Viking merchants did not give coins different values as we do today. They measured them purely by weight, using folding scales like these from tenth-century York. A trader might offer half a coin or a lump of silver chopped from a bracelet as change! Viking traders would agree a sale by slapping hands.

◀ The collapse of the **Frankish Empire** after its powerful emperor Charlemagne died in 814, provided rich pickings for the Vikings. They traded and raided at the same time, taking home cloth, pottery, wine, weapons and luxury items like this ninth-century silver cup found in Denmark.

International ▶ markets like Birka – where this tenth-century crucifix was found – attracted the first Christian **missionaries** and churches. Vikings often agreed to become Christians purely so that Christian merchants would trade with them!

# SETTLERS

From Norway, Viking ships explored west across the Atlantic. In 982 Vikings settled in Greenland. Then, according to the Sagas, Leif the Lucky's followers landed in Vinland. Viking tools recently discovered at L'Anse aux Meadows, Newfoundland, show that Vinland was in fact America – the Vikings reached it five hundred years before Columbus.

The Vikings arrived in Iceland around 860. Glad to escape from the harsh rule of their king, Harald Finehair, many of them settled there. When Leif the Lucky's father, Eirik the Red, was banished from Iceland for murder, he voyaged even further across the Atlantic. He discovered Greenland, and in 986 founded a colony which survived for five hundred years. Its remains, at Brattahlid, are shown here.

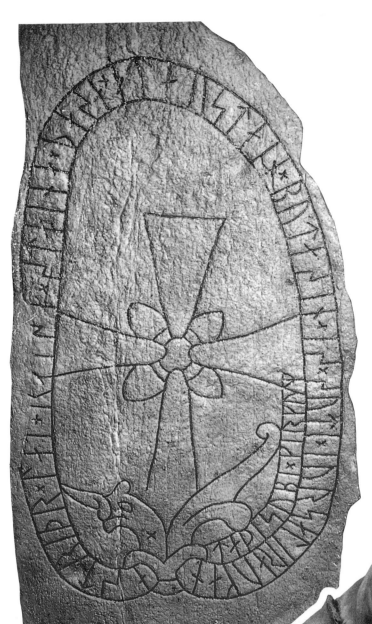

◄ Many Vikings travelled east in search of the fabulous wealth of Constantinople, the capital of the **Byzantine Empire**. Byzantine emperors formed the Vikings into their own personal army called the Varangian Guard. Rune stones like this one from Broby, Sweden, record the deaths of many Viking soldiers in the east: 'Estrid had this stone erected in memory of Osten, her husband, who went to Jerusalem and died in Greece'.

The rich farmlands of Britain encouraged the Viking raiders to settle down and form *colonies*. They settled in the islands off the coast of Scotland, in the Isle of Man and in Ireland. In 867 they captured the city we now call York, which they named Jorvik. This Viking boot was found there. Jorvik became the capital of the Viking kingdom of Northumbria. ▼

13

# THE VIKING PEOPLE

**Most Vikings were land-owners called bondirs or carls, who lived on family farms served by slaves called *thralls*. Above them were local chieftains called jarls, or earls. The most powerful Vikings were the royal families of Denmark, Norway and Sweden, the separate kingdoms in which Vikings lived.**

Local assemblies, called **things**, controlled law and order. Vikings in Iceland formed Europe's earliest national parliament, the **Althing**. This parliament met every year, here at Thingvellir, which means Parliament Plains. A law-speaker would mount the 'law-rock' to announce decisions, such as Iceland's conversion to Christianity in the year 1000. ▼

▲ Women ran the Viking farms while their husbands were at sea. The woman's importance in the family was shown by the household keys, like the one shown here. She hung the keys from her belt. She had the right to divorce her husband if he kept these keys from her!

Craftsmen like carpenters and wood-carvers were highly respected in Viking society. These tools, which have modern handles, belonged to a Viking wood-worker of Mastermyr, Gotland. They would have been used for ship-building. ▼

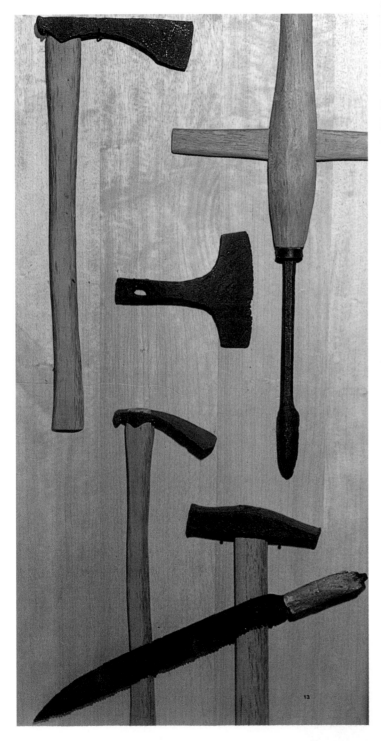

▲ The most valued craftsman was the blacksmith, who forged tools, weapons, nails and locks, using the **anvil**, hammer and tongs which today's smiths still use. This twelfth-century church carving, illustrating the Viking **myth** of Sigurd the Dragon-Slayer, shows Regin the Smith forging a sword strong enough to split his anvil.

# DAILY LIFE

Archaeologists have discovered Viking remains of ploughed fields, farm tools, animal bones and even fishing tackle. These show that the Vikings were very efficient farmers, who could produce all the food they needed. They grew wheat and produced meat and dairy products. They also caught fish and wild animals to eat.

A typical family ate, slept and worked in a single, rectangular hall or long-house. Its walls were made of timber sealed with moss, or wattle and daub (woven twigs covered with clay). The house had a sloping roof that was thatched or turfed. Inside, sleeping benches ran along the walls, and a central hearth beneath a smoke-hole supplied light, warmth and heat for cooking. This is a reconstruction of houses and wooden paths at the Viking town of Hedeby in Denmark.

▲ The Vikings used wooden bowls, spoons and knives and many other kitchen utensils, like these from York. Their diet included fish and meat, which were salted and dried for long winters or sea voyages. They also ate cabbages, peas, oats and fruits. Food was sweetened with honey, flavoured by garlic and spices, and washed down with large amounts of beer!

Every girl was ▶ taught to use a hand-spindle. This was a weighted rod which spun thread from wool. The wool was dyed, and woven on *looms* into cloth for clothing and sails. Linen, made from the plant flax, was smoothed on whale-bone 'ironing boards' like this one.

# APPEARANCE

**An Arab trader called Ibn Fadlan wrote of Viking men's appearance in 922: 'I have never seen more perfect physical specimens, tall as date palms, blond and ruddy'. Most wore beards, often parted in the middle, like that which gave Danish king Svein Forkbeard his name.**

Viking men commonly wore a belted, buttonless tunic beneath a cloak of fur or brightly-dyed cloth. This was fastened at one shoulder by a ring-and-pin brooch, leaving the sword-arm free. Trousers were either tight like today's ski-pants, flared, or very baggy. Both sexes wore leather shoes, with hats and gloves of leather or wool.

This tenth-century brooch was discovered at Hornelund in Denmark. It shows the skill of Viking goldsmiths. The fine gold thread decoration is called filigree. Poorer people wore cheap copies of such jewellery, which were mass-produced. ▼

◄ To show off their wealth, Viking traders had silver coins melted down to make jewellery for their wives, like this beautiful bracelet from Denmark.

This Swedish pendant shows how a Viking ► woman dressed. She wore a long, pleated linen dress, beneath two cloth rectangles hung from shoulder straps which were fastened by oval brooches. A shawl, held at the throat by a winged or drum-shaped brooch, was thought fashionable. Necklaces of glass beads were common. A married woman covered her hair-knot with a head scarf.

# BURIAL

**The Vikings either *cremated* or buried their dead. They were buried with their finest possessions – for use in the afterlife. Many of these grave goods provide us with information about Viking life. Ships, so important in life, even carried the dead to the next world. Gravestones were set out in the shape of a ship. Kings and queens were buried beneath burial mounds containing slaughtered slaves and animals, and entire longships.**

The richest grave was discovered at Oseberg in 1904. It contained this beautiful 21-metre long ship, and the furniture of a royal household. Two skeletons found with it are possibly those of Queen Asa, grandmother of Harald Finehair, and her *sacrificed* slave. Note the carved stern and the rudder or steer-board, from which the word *starboard* comes.

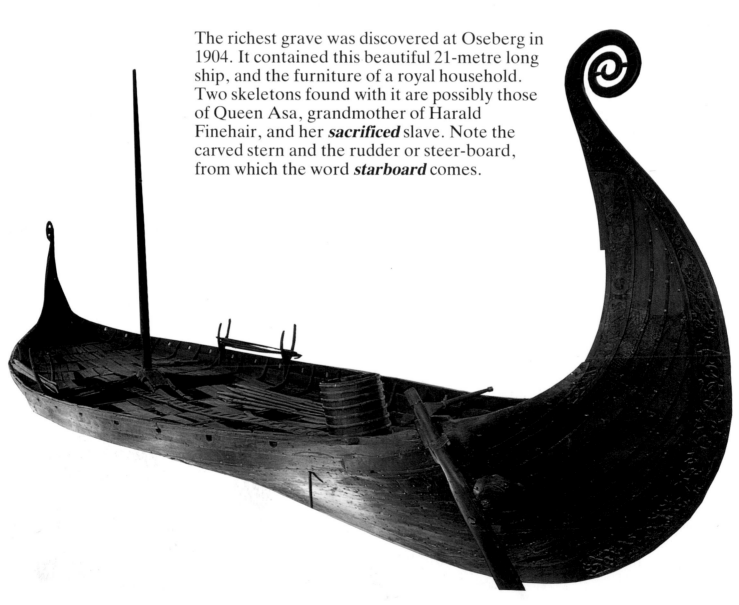

▲ The Oseberg burial contained the finest examples of Viking carving. This dragon's-head post was intended to frighten away evil spirits. It is covered with nightmarish creatures called gripping beasts, which often appear in Viking art.

▲ Also found at Oseberg were a wagon, kitchen equipment, the skeletons of at least ten horses, riding gear, beds, chests, looms, tapestries and an ox! The style of this figure, which decorates a fine bucket found at Oseberg, shows that it originally came from Ireland.

◄ This carving of a mythical hero in a snake-pit appears on one of four sledges dug up at Oseberg. Sledges were an important form of travel during Scandinavia's long winters.

# RELIGION

**The Vikings followed an ancient religion. They worshipped a race of gods called the Aesir. Tales of the incredible adventures of these gods were told by generations of Viking poets called skalds, and written down in the Sagas of thirteenth-century Iceland.**

Odin was the god of war and poetry. His warrior-maidens, called **valkyries**, led the spirits of Viking warriors killed in battle to Valhalla, the Hall of the Slain. This was a place of constant feasting and fighting. The picture-stone shows, top left, three slain warriors with down-pointed swords approaching Valhalla. Odin's eight-legged horse, Sleipnir, carries a fourth warrior.

Thor was the mighty, red-bearded thunder god. He fought with a magical hammer against his enemies the Giants. Many Vikings carried charms, like this tenth-century Thor's hammer, to summon Thor's protection. Note the silver coils which represent Thor's staring eyes. The word 'Thursday' originally meant 'Thor's day'. ▼

▲ This tapestry from a church in Sweden, shows three gods: (from left to right) the one-eyed Odin; Thor with his hammer; and Frey, god of *fertility*, holding an ear of corn. Human sacrifices were offered to these three gods at a Viking temple in Old Uppsala in Sweden.

23

# WAR

**The Vikings were most famous as warriors. They used weapons that were better than any that had been used before, and followed a religion that encouraged them to be fearless. Vikings hated to die from old age – known as 'a straw death'. Dying in battle, though, offered the chance of going to glorious Valhalla.**

Viking warriors did not wear the horned helmets often wrongly shown in films. In fact they wore plain, conical helmets – like the ones on these Norse chessmen from the Isle of Lewis, Scotland. The figure biting his shield represents a '***berserk***'. This was a much-feared warrior who furiously attacked his enemies, wearing no armour but a bear or wolf-skin, and howling like a beast. From this behaviour comes the expression, 'Gone berserk'.

Spears and bows ▶ were used, but the most popular weapon was the sword. Viking craftsmen added strong blades – traded from the Frankish Empire – to hilts of wood, horn or precious metal. So deadly were these blades in Viking hands that the Franks forbade their sale! Warriors gave their swords names like 'Leg Biter' and 'Golden Hilted', which might describe this weapon from Sweden.

▲ The deadly broad-bladed battle axe was the symbol of Viking terror. Olaf the Stout named his axe 'Hel' after the goddess of the dead. King Knut of Denmark allowed only axe-men to join his bodyguard. This tenth-century iron axe-head from Mammen in Denmark has a serpent design beautifully inlaid into it with silver.

# THE INVADERS

**By 870, Viking invaders had conquered most of England. Only Wessex, ruled by Alfred the Great, resisted them. Alfred signed a treaty called the Danelaw, giving the north of England to the Vikings. Similarly, lands in France were granted to the giant Viking Hrolf (or Rollo) and named Normandy.**

When Ethelred became King of England in 978 he tried to buy peace by giving the Vikings payments of silver called '*Danegeld*'. Such easy loot only encouraged Viking kings to return with larger armies. In 1018 Vikings received nearly 37,500 kilograms of Danegeld, including coins like these – one of which shows King Ethelred.

This is a page from the Anglo-Saxon Chronicles, in which English writers recorded the terror of 'the force' – the Vikings. Even the nursery rhyme *London Bridge is falling down* recalls a Viking attack, when in 1010 Olaf the Stout's oarsmen fixed cables from their longships to London Bridge and dragged it down into the Thames. ▼

▲ In 1016 Knut Sveinsson, son of Svein Forkbeard, became the first Viking king of all England. Like many later Vikings, Knut was a Christian. He once commanded the ocean waves to turn back, to show that even a king was ruled by God. The waves kept coming, and Knut proved that only God is all-powerful. Knut died in 1035, having successfully ruled an empire including England, Denmark, Norway and part of Sweden.

# DOOMSDAY OF THE GODS

**The Vikings always believed the gods they worshipped would be destroyed at 'Ragnarok' – 'Doomsday of the Gods' – and that Odin would be eaten by his enemy, Fenrir the Wolf. In fact, the downfall of their gods, and the end of the Viking Age itself, came with the spread of Christianity throughout Scandinavia.**

In 1066 the last great Viking, Harald Hardrada, King of Norway, was defeated at Stamford Bridge by England's King Harold Godwinsson – whose own name is a Viking one. Two days later, another Viking descendant, William of Normandy, invaded England. He crossed the Channel in the longships shown here on the **Bayeux Tapestry** and conquered England at the Battle of Hastings.

Rulers like William the Conqueror built up defences and armies to end the great Viking raids. Vikings who had settled abroad were generally absorbed into the native population. Many reminders of the Viking Age remain, like this warrior laid out with his weapons for pagan burial, carved on a tenth century cross at Middleton in Yorkshire, England.
▼

▲ Having once looted Lindisfarne's monastery, the Vikings then built their own churches, like this one at Borgund in Norway. It is called a stave-church, after the upright planks or staves which construct its walls. As well as crosses, it is decorated with fierce dragons'-heads to scare the old Viking gods away!

29

# GLOSSARY

**Althing**   The national parliament of Iceland.

**Anvil**   A heavy iron block on which metals are hammered into shape.

**Archaeologist**   Someone who studies objects and remains from past civilizations.

**Artefacts**   Objects, such as tools or pots, that archaeologists study to find out how people used to live.

**Bayeux Tapestry**   A famous work of embroidery showing William the Conqueror's invasion of England.

**Berserk**   Wild, fighting-mad warrior.

**Byzantine Empire**   The Roman Empire in the East, whose capital was Constantinople.

**Colony**   A settlement in a new country.

**Cremated**   Burnt a corpse.

**Danegeld**   A tax in England which raised money to pay off Vikings.

**Empire**   Foreign lands controlled by a country or emperor.

**Fertility**   The ability for people to have children and for land to produce crops.

**Figurehead**   Carving on the front of a ship.

**Fjord**   A long, narrow sea inlet between high cliffs.

**Frankish Empire**   The empire centred around Germany from about 400 to 850.

**Keel**   The lowest beam of a ship, on which the rest of the ship's frame is built.

**Looms**   Machines for weaving thread into cloth.

**Minted**   Made metal into coins.

**Missionaries**   Travelling religious preachers.

**Myths**   Stories about heroes or gods.

**Ragnarok**   The predicted day of the Viking gods' destruction.

**Relics**   Objects remaining from an earlier time.

**Sacrifice**   To kill people or animals as offerings to a goddess or god.

**Scandinavia**   Group name for Denmark, Norway, Sweden and Iceland.

**Starboard**   The right-hand side of a ship.

**Thing**   Public law-making assembly of Vikings.

**Thrall**   A Viking slave, who was not allowed to carry weapons.

**Tradition**   A custom or practice passed on from one generation to another.

**Valkyries**   Beautiful maidens who served the god Odin by taking the spirits of dead heroes to Valhalla.

**Vane**   A flat metal blade that shows which way the wind is blowing.

# IMPORTANT DATES

**793** Vikings raid Lindisfarne
**835** First Danish invasion of England
**860** Vikings discover Iceland
**867** York (Jorvik) in England captured by Vikings
**886** Alfred the Great signs Peace of Wedmore, establishing Danelaw
**911** Hrolf (Rollo) receives Normandy from French King Charles the Simple
**982** Eirik the Red discovers Greenland
**984-1014** Svein Forkbeard reigns as king of Denmark
**986** Leif the Lucky lands in America

**995-1000** Olaf Tryggvason reigns as king of Norway
**1000** Iceland adopts Christianity
**1010** Olaf the Stout pulls down London Bridge
**1015-1030** Olaf the Stout rules Norway
**1016-1035** Knut rules as first Viking king of all England
**1047-1066** Harald Hardrada reigns as king of Norway
**1066** Harald Hardrada killed at Stamford Bridge
William of Normandy conquers England
**1200s** The Sagas are written in Iceland

# BOOKS TO READ

**The Vikings** by Michael Gibson (Macdonald, 1976)
This is a good, illustrated introduction to the study of the Vikings.

**Viking Explorers** by Rupert Matthews (Wayland, 1989)
An illustrated book that deals with the travels of the Vikings.

**Viking Invaders and Settlers** by Tony D Triggs (Wayland, 1992)
A very useful book for learning about the effect the Vikings had on Britain.

**Vikings** (I Was There series) by J D Clare (Bodley Head, 1991)
This book is full of excellent photographs of reconstructed Viking scenes, giving an idea of what Viking life looked like.

**The Viking World** by J Graham-Campbell (Frances Lincoln, 1980)
This larger book is ideal for anyone who wishes to study the Vikings in more detail.

# INDEX